SELF-PORTRAITS IN WHICH I DO NOT APPEAR

poems by

Clif Mason

Finishing Line Press
Georgetown, Kentucky

SELF-PORTRAITS
IN WHICH
I DO NOT APPEAR

Copyright © 2020 by Clif Mason
ISBN 978-1-64662-179-8 First Edition
All rights reserved under International and Pan-American Copyright Conventions. No part of this book may be reproduced in any manner whatsoever without written permission from the publisher, except in the case of brief quotations embodied in critical articles and reviews.

ACKNOWLEDGMENTS

I am grateful to the editors of these magazines and newspapers, in whose pages versions of these poems appeared:

Bacopa Literary Review
By&By Poetry
Metropolitan
Negative Capability
Passager
Peacock Journal

I would also like to thank members of my writing group, with whom I shared early drafts of some of these poems: Brown Lyles, Katie Berger, Cat Dixon, Trent Walters, Fran Higgins, Shyla Punteney, Britny Cordera, Genevieve Williams, and Laura Madeline Wiseman. Thanks always to Laurie, the first reader of these poems.

Special gratitude to Leah Maines, Christen Kincaid, and all of the wonderful staff at Finishing Line Press.

Publisher: Leah Maines
Editor: Christen Kincaid
Cover Art: Laurie E. Mason
Author Photo: Laurie E. Mason
Cover Design: Elizabeth Maines McCleavy

Printed in the USA on acid-free paper.
Order online: www.finishinglinepress.com
   also available on amazon.com

Author inquiries and mail orders:
Finishing Line Press
P. O. Box 1626
Georgetown, Kentucky 40324
U. S. A.

Table of Contents

[As simple as the stars] 1

[She lay down in a long lagoon of hours] 2

[Radioactive coral, pearl sprung from the shoulder] 4

[She was tracked by the lion of her becoming] 5

[Did he live in the unreal] 6

[She was an amethyst ear in the midsummer dark] 7

[He rang a bell made of woven twigs] 8

[She had reason to speak of winter] 10

[When he dived off the trestle of the railroad bridge] 11

[She solved the rebus of the spider's web] 12

[People stood in the street] 14

[It was the summer she kept walking] 16

[If wishes were windows and every witch] 17

[Between the spine of glass and the face of leaves] 18

[Twilight knew his shape] 20

[She spent her days in a golden tent and all the circus people loved her] 21

[The moon drugged the sea with its milky light] 22

[School days were filled with naysayers] 23

[Every morning the rivers forgot their names] 24

Note 26

like the stars
at the streaming boundaries of unlivable gold
Alice Rahon, "Pointed Out Like the Stars"

[As simple as the stars]

As simple as the stars,
which were not simple at all.
As ruined as the rain,

which only appeared clear and pure.
As damaged as the dead fox.
Yes, just that damaged.

What did anyone know of others' stories,
and who, if anyone, would tell them?
Some assumed they were stories of compassion,

some of cruelty.
How could their questions best be answered?
When did they realize it wasn't answers they sought?

Last night they dreamed five dreams.
Today they seemed more real than their lives.
They slept to wake, only to sleep again.

Birdsong was their guide, and wind chimes—
all things singing, all songs sung.
Lightning burned their eyes.

They were no longer blind.

[She lay down in a long lagoon of hours]

She lay down in a long lagoon of hours,
                                  where light was iced,
               silent,
       in an emerald.
As summer printed its last bees,
                               algae spread
           its green kimono across the lake
                 and days swirled away,
             ghostly as the smoke of leaf fires.

She broke into stunning sun
                          after days of water
             running into the fissures
       and forgotten crypts of the earth,
               of the clack and clatter
         of seafarer birds.

Gulls whispered
             in willing ears
                 and shorelines dissolved
       behind wings.

Her pinions seized
                 the invisible.
She was not made
                   for anything less.

Nights of the union
                   of anthracite
                           and cloud.
Flesh burned up like a falling star,
                          sizzling
             in the dark overhead.

Ah, the sad percussion
                        of flower heads,
        as they beat themselves seedless
                                and ragged
                against the jaws
        of desolate machines.

When fireflies beckoned, calling
                in their chemical code of love,
        words' arterial blood pummeled
                                in temples,
                        smeared and smirched
        the star-white page,
                        livid as fresh clots.

When death's dusk and darkness
                                was forsworn
        but not defeated,
                she stood as one sliced in the brain,
                        illness-
                bewildered.
Still, she held herself upright,
                                breathed,
                momentarily charmed
                        by the delusion of strength.
She was fading, perceptibly fading.

One day she would faint, wearied,
                        as the world wearied
        and weakened
                        all living things,
                until they fell into the deep,
                        deep arms
        of dearest death—
                        not cold as often thought,
                                but warm,
                welcoming and warm.

[Radioactive coral, pearl sprung from the shoulder}

Radioactive coral, pearl sprung from the shoulder
of night's chancery. The square root of air was coal,
a star of ice, a million mutations of the possible.
The indistinct river became distinct and the eye's
torpedo exploded the random number generator
in the gray cranium of the ordinary.

Night after night his ghosts drank from the goblet
of rancor and razorblades, of repentance and regret,
in a room frosted with cold moonlight.
They couldn't breathe in the helium of their distance.
As tenderness drained like blood from their faces,
disappointment flowed in to replace it.
A ceibo red as arterial blood turned brown and died.

A ruffled blue sheaf of feathers—the swallow-
tailed manakin stared hard into day's first light
as a voice spoke from the battlements of air.

Are you the person, hapless and hopeless,
blown out of a plane blown out of the sky,
the geographer of a mute certainty,
the will of a catapult? If so, you are one I seek,
and it is fortune itself that has brought you to me
through this long and labyrinthine journey.

He wanted to answer, but the voice was gone.
The speech joined the hundreds of others like it
in the museum of unfinished conversations.

[She was tracked by the lion of her becoming]

She was tracked
    by the lion
        of her becoming.
Sometimes she wanted to escape it.
       Sometimes she didn't.
  The lion took its time,
      crossed
         any water
    or desert,
traveled any distance.

  Was she walking away from
        or towards it?
She didn't fear it.
    How could she
        if she didn't know
    what it was?

  She strolled through lime
      and avocado trees,
followed a double hook in the path,
        and there it stood.
    Its growl was guttural
and raw and deep,
    concussing the air
      like tiny landmines.

  They leaped
        and fused
     in mid-air,
    like a star newborn and golden,
burning,
      filling the night with a light
    it had never known,
       singing in a language
the world had never heard.
    The lion shook its head
       and stood up,
         a woman.

[Did he live in the unreal]

Did he live in the unreal
as if it were no more unsettling
than the routine?
Did he sing, though his voice
box was broken?
Crows damaged the sky
and deer lay down with wolves.
It was important to know what was
happening. It could not be stopped
but it could be altered.
Did he walk, without hesitating,
through a door, black as space,
that opened, successively,
on a pod of whales,
a great crater on the moon,
a desert like a lion's golden hide,
a house in which no one was home
but music filled the air,
a library shelved with books
that hadn't been written yet,
and a theater stage
on which a play was performed,
a play in which he was invited
to see waves crashing
against a landlocked city
or trees floating
like green feathers in the air?

[She was an amethyst ear in the midsummer dark]

She was an amethyst ear in the midsummer dark. Bodies seeped anguish and grief, and she heard them fill up. Star upon star. Enough to make her worship obsidian night and start raucous ceremonies of clairvoyance. When the night air touched her like down, she shivered, not cold but awake to the river and to the moon, holding its breath as it swam for miles underwater.

Hers could be a basalt courage, repulsing each assault, building always toward some fresh, some irrevocable, reversal and renewal. She danced with the revelers and joined the souls leaping from body to body. The rain was rain, nothing more. The wind was wind, nothing less. Hail's hammers struck the earth and lightning turned trees into kindling. Before her birth, her mother knew this and passed it into her blood.

Disappointment clotted in the arteries of those who let it, and thousands were dispatched each day in just that slow and lethal way. In the alleys of the dispossessed, she found sand and black ice, and her skin was abraded by rawhide and rivets. Since all humor was gallows humor, she wondered if the dark energy of the universe were not life. For this world was infinitely clever and canny, and the intricacy of the merest mite of a smidge could shake the assurance of even the most quick-witted.

She asked, *What light is this that turns my face blue in the castle of the dead?* She spat hard seeds from her mouth, swallowed brackish water. At night, a star's skin became bagpipe music. During the day it was rice paper. Air was barely functional. Well water caused strange dreams. Butterflies languished, carpeting the demeanor of noon, and risk-averse mice slept in rooms deep and cool.

She had a hankering to embroider herself onto time's handkerchief. Only poems were free, and clouds and the kisses of first and enduring love. Emerald and quartz tropes, facets of a reality that broke light and broke it again. Gesturing hands printed the air. Perhaps words would last longer, *impress* more.

[He rang a bell made of woven twigs]

        He rang a bell
                        made of woven twigs
and the music stayed with him
                              all night.
        Walking one day
with a tall horse,
            he filled his ears
                      with many sentences.

        Hummingbirds hovered,
                drinking from the ground cloud
wrapped round
        the bushes and trees.

        When the fog burned off,
chorus frogs swore vows
                    of silence
          and blue dragonflies
practiced takeoffs and landings
                for hours.

        He asked directions of a bumblebee.
It said, *Remember your middle name*
            and the day your mother was born.
        As bee imperatives went,
this one,
            it seemed to him,
                        was less gnomic
            and more transparent
        than most.

    The task was not to do well
                        the often achieved,
            but to attempt
what had never been.

    The tinkling of glass—
                was that the world shattering
or the breaking of a snow globe
                      slipped from the hand
        and impeded only by air?

    He mimed his own unsuspecting walk
                            onto void,
        certain the nothing
would buoy him up,
    and he would
                not only survive but thrive:
An invisible path would rise
                      to meet his feet.

    Was this a story
                with no characters
      or characters with no story?
The answer wasn't readily apparent.

[She had reason to speak of winter]

She had reason to speak of winter
                              even in mid-
                        summer,
    to feel ice on her sweating brow.
Icicles hung, motionless chimes,
        stinging tongues of frost,
                          chanting poems
            that became hawks and owls,
                  hunting the haunted fields.

If she scalpeled off the face the world knew,
                          she saw—
    one person's heart was a magazine
                        of shells,
        another was a mile of wrecked cars.
An unsuspecting diver was suspended mid-
                                arc.

The past was an obelisk,
                        a crime.
What happened inside the skin factory?
        Her feet were nailed to their prints
        and rancor was inevitable.

She was a strong sidereal heartbeat,
            radioing through time's dark body,
    flesh leafing out,
            flowering bold as a star
on a white stalk of bone.

She wakened in daybreak clouds
                the color of hyacinth macaws
    and black swans,
        in spark and spill of blaze,
            in sprays of praise and mirth,
      in solar flaring
and sweet nimbus-burn,
            until time blew us to rags
        and laid us down in the earth,
                our common grave.

[When he dived off the trestle of the railroad bridge]

When he dived off the trestle of the railroad bridge, he gashed his head on a mostly submerged log and knocked himself out. Three friends jumped in and dragged him to shore and gave him mouth-to-mouth in the weeds and muddy clay, as gnats and mosquitoes fogged up. When he came to, they drove him in Terry's Camaro to the E.R. The doctor sent him home, his skull all Frankensteined on one side, with strict orders to rest. He wasn't supposed to drink but he sent them out for beer—and with a message for the girlfriend waiting to hear from him. He sat in front of the window air conditioner, feeling cold air flow over his bandage like the by then black current of the river he'd tried his level best to dive into because water ever sought water and everything that was was one dark flowing.

[She solved the rebus of the spider's web]

She solved the rebus of the spider's web
            and she balanced
                        and bounced
                on something
        light as air,
ballasted by those
                who accompanied her.

She breathed and her blood
                  brightened
        and her mouth bloomed,
                    a rose
        in a garden of faces.

Did she ride the white water engine
        over rocks and stumps,
                and drink from stalactites
     in a cavern's heart?

She burned the mountain
                    until the lamp
        glowed in the charcoal
    of the moment,
                  gleamed like glass
        as it melted
and returned to the shore
            on which she stood
                    singing—
     and the song swept out
from words
              on a torn scrap of paper,
    and the blood raced
        with the song,
                    flaming

as it flowed, until the song
        was the blood
and the blood was the song,
      flaming as it raced
         from the land
    to the sea
  to the stars
       to the single point
     that was the song
and the blood that was
        the beginning
    and the end
and the beginning
      of everything.

[People stood in the street]

        People stood in the street.
Had they forgotten
                where they were going?
        When the owls called,
    they rolled the moon
                back and forth
        between them.
The city wanted to drink
                from the clouds,
    so they had rain for a week.

        Notes pulled themselves
                from staves
and ran off quickly as they could.
        What did people do
                without music?
Some noticed right off.
                Others took years.
    The apples didn't feel at home
on the earth,
        so they flew back
                onto the branches.

        When the notes returned,
springing up
        like mushrooms,
            there was much feasting,
      and people sang—
               alone,
                    in duets,
in choruses as great
        as the city itself.
                Even the crows grew weary
of their caws
        and signed up for singing lessons.

　　　　The snow did not remember
　　　　　　　　　　　　　　its name,
so it went around asking every stranger.
　　　　　　　A door opened into a birdcall,
　　　　into a lake we could not see across.
It opened into leaves
　　　　　　　that never raised their voices
　　　　　　　　　　　　　　above a whisper,
　　　　into shadows bright as the sun.
　　　　　　　　　Why did they ask more?
More was killing them
　　　　　　　　　　one note at a time.

[It was the summer she kept walking]

It was the summer she kept walking
out of disappointment
and into something more.
Not success exactly,
and not victory,
but something more,
like the rose thorn she gripped.

She endured a second
until the magic took hold,
and, in an instant's reversal of field,
she pierced the thorn.
She pointed at the air and spun about
and there was rain.
She smacked the river
and there was flood.

She knew that one day,
if she said star,
a new star would condense
from a nebula's hot gas,
condense until it glowed and burned
and burst with unquenchable fusion—
and a new light adorned the darkness.

and when she knew that,
it was nothing to persist.
She wore discipline like a new dress.

She could see her future as clearly
as others could see the present.

[If wishes were windows and every witch]

If wishes were windows and every witch
rode a horse of song and dreams,
the cold zero of night would not provoke
envy in flaming day and stars would not
yearn to be seed fluffs careering
in the breeze like escaped kites.
Drops rained through freezing air, and ice
reigned supreme. The secret was to exist
wholly without secrets. When tracked
by the lion of despair, besieged
by the fire ants of self-interest, gripped
by the teeth of the grizzly bear of deceit,
he thought of her, wings burst from his back,
and pinions burned through the air between them.

[Between the spine of glass and the face of leaves]

                  Between the spine of glass
                                  and the face of leaves,
the green veil
                      and the sleeping violin,
        night smothered day
                              beneath its black pillow.

                  Constellations rose,
hoarfrost on jet sky,
                      and two humpback whales
                                        slept,
                    vertical heads
      only a foot off the ocean floor,
galleons looming
                  in black fathoms.

                  Some days she wailed
                                  and wept,
            like the moon
    with broken ribs,
                          or she sang,
like the desert
              dreaming it is a sea.
        She taught her song
                          to a morning glory,
     and then there were
              two of them
         to weep and sing.

                        Between the broken candle
and the silk curtains,
                        the gold leaf
                                    and the galloping horse,
        she read from the diary
                                    of barred owl nights,
and poems took flight,
                        commanded the air.

                    She dreamt the world
                                    around her,
wove it
                like a cloak of petals.
            Did the moon,
conversant in many languages,
                                    intercede for her
                    with the wind?
                Words questioned
their ordinary meanings
                            and deserted
        the dictionary of portents.

                    She was not
                                a floating dandelion seed.
        No,
                she was a great blue heron,
        migrating undaunted,
                            day after day,
against even the most punishing
                                        of winds.

[Twilight knew his shape]

Twilight knew his shape
She drew it in her sketchbook
of phantoms and covert dreams—
swiftly but with shadowed depth
and detail, for purposes
she didn't, or wouldn't, confide.
It was illusion making,
and masking, illusion.

Illusion drew phantoms
and knew their covert dreams.
He sketched swiftly
in his book of dark pages.
The detail belied
his shadowy purposes.
He convinced twilight
to confide in him, promising
never to unmask her.

He drew a hundred illusions
in his bright notebook of masks
Covert dreams confided in him.
He took phantoms
and made them look,
as was his purpose,
like nothing less
than twilight itself.
The detail was so precise
it convinced everyone.

[She spent her days in a golden tent and all the circus people loved her]

She spent her days in a golden tent and all the circus people loved her. Those were her favorite stories. It wasn't easy to convince people, but she had a gift for the details—the brown stains on the tiger's teeth, the shackle scars on the elephants' legs, the black bear's doggy snout, the male lion's notched ear.

Depending on her whim or mood, she'd been a wirewalker or equestrian, a trapeze artist or ropedancer. As she spoke, she saw the tent perfectly—its guy-wires taut, its canvas billowing, its doorway tempting to small birds seeking a place to roost. In a green pasture, on a sunny day, the tent looked like a radiant cloud.

[The moon drugged the sea with its milky light]

The moon drugged the sea with its milky light, and all of the fish were enspelled. Sharks left off eating. Dolphins rested on wave crests, dreaming. The water was sleek and sick with warm opaline light.

As gulls drowned and turtles sank, giant squid stretched tentacles toward unknown depths. Meteors sizzled like lucifers dropped into water, and the earth drifted, drifted, inert as the victim of some random beating.

He thought he'd known grief. He'd known nothing.

The ocean was bedazzled by alabaster light. The shattered ship descended into the blacker waters below, a nothing swallowed by a vaster nothing.

He lay suspended on the cold and pallid waves, spared but unforgiven, forsaken. He waited, waited for the preposterous, the impossible—for the dawn to break and the ship of some mercy to appear and bear toward him.

[School days were filled with naysayers]

School days were filled with naysayers,
with adults who saw only
out the backs of their heads,
whose mouths moved but the words
came from their bellybuttons, garbled
and sounding like 45 records played
at 33 1/3, whose hands grasped
everything good but dropped it all,
filling the air with broken promises.

What did she do when the world
was always telling her *no*,
was always saying, *You're wrong,*
the rain is not spiraling
strips of melting taffy,
the moon is not a giant that looked
at a gorgon and was turned to stone,
and the stars are most certainly not
fistfuls of gravel flung into the air?

How did she keep standing up
when bullies knocked her down
and ripped her new skirt and stole
her library book, though she knew
they didn't like to read
and would just tear it up and throw
it in a dumpster in some alley?
How did she keep getting up
and following them and gathering

all the torn pieces against her chest,
until the words flowed through
her skin and into her heart,
and were held there for years, until,
one day they were recreated—
in new thoughts, in different
lines—and were spoken
by the woman she had,
against all odds, become?

[Every morning the rivers forgot their names]

Every morning the rivers forgot their names,
so he gave them new ones, names of sleek,
sibilant sounds. The rain chanted the names,
and the daybreak birds celebrated them from all sides,
until the stones hummed and the daylily
and carnation petals whispered them
We were creatures made for joy, though the world
delivered the mail of sadness to our door.

He walked around the neighborhood, talking to himself,
muttering the words of invisibility and suspending the law
of gravity. He heard dance music from the country.
of childhood. On the street desperate men sold knives
made of blue air. No one knew they'd been cut
until they collapsed with a shirt full of blood.

What did he say beneath a cadmium comet,
facing the buffets of a phosphorus wind?
Did he choose to sing the ballad of the inconsolable,
heat-stroked with loss, or to chant good luck charms
for the destitute? Or did he go further and fill the air
with waterspouts and floating labyrinths? He didn't ask
others the nature of his task. He simply sang
threads of light into night's ocean, silent fins
dividing dark waves. He sang until his fingers
turned to glass and shimmered when he held them up
to moonlight. He beat unknown rhythms
on the tympani of verbs and let the trumpets of nouns
announce themselves and parade through scales.
Words became the mongoose that seized the cobra,
the wolverine that stood down the polar bear.

What could still be said, after so many lines,
so many lifetimes. *Plant trees and poems,
hardiest of perennials. Always face bracing winds,
kiss warm lips. Every moment is a flower and a star,
and this life both a garden and a galaxy.
A great deal can yet be done
if you put your whole body to the task.*

Note

The epigraph is from a translation by Myrna Bell Rochester. The poem can be found in *Surrealist Women: An International Anthology*, edited by Penelope Rosemont.

Clif Mason lives in Bellevue, Nebraska, with his wife, a visual artist. He is the author of the poetry collections, *Knocking the Stars Senseless* and *From the Dead Before*. He is also the Dean of the College of Arts and Sciences at Bellevue University. His job is to help faculty create the programs of study that will enable students to become the most complete human beings they can become and to do important work in the larger service of the community. He sees his work as a dean and a poet as continuous.

Clif Mason's poems have appeared in many magazines in America and England, including *Evergreen Review, Southern Poetry Review, New Millennium Writings, The New Guard, Poet Lore, Orbis,* and *Iota*. He is fortunate that his work has been awarded prizes by the Joe Gouveia Outermost Poetry Contest (chosen by Marge Piercy), *Writers' Journal, Plainsongs,* the Midwest Writers' Conference, and the Academy of American Poets. His work has been nominated for a Pushcart Prize and he has been the recipient of a Fulbright Fellowship to Rwanda, Africa.

www.ingramcontent.com/pod-product-compliance
Lightning Source LLC
LaVergne TN
LVHW041517070426
835507LV00012B/1629